# I Didn't Mean To...

Pooja Hiremath

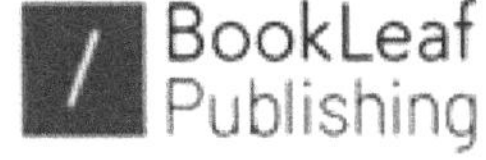

Presentation by *BookLeaf Publishing*

Web: www.bookleafpub.com

E-mail: info@bookleafpub.com

ISBN : 9789357210096

First edition 2022

# DEDICATION

To Bobby, for inspiring me write again and begin again a new chapter.

# ACKNOWLEDGEMENT

Thank you Amma. You are my first reader. Without your support, I wouldn't have the courage to continue to write. Thank you Chit. Our numerous chats full of philosophy and laughter help me find my revelations and the right words to express myself. Thank you Richie, for all our years of friendship, I wouldn't be who I am without you.

# PREFACE

goodbye
loathed I am
as the end to ventures
my candied partings leave
a bitter aftertaste
I'm shunned for my misnomer.
an unfair persecution
for my birthright occupation
I'm no less than
Hello awkwardly smiling
at passing strangers
I'm no different than
Thank You forcibly gracious
to unwanted assistance.
in the end, I do favors
acknowledging the
value of your presence -
without me, the finality,
the partially ajar concoctions
of what ifs will haunt

## propose

ambivalent I was not, jumping in with two feet
beyond doubt we were endgame,was I
crazy two weeks in? my first relationship
desperately, I wanted us to survive the
ephemeral college romance trope. but my
father and you were dissonant men in my life
given the choice between the two
hands down, I'd always choose you -
I never thought always would change.
just when I made strides to leave behind
kiddom, striking independence from family
leveled the playing field you did
marriage, a down the road, you said
not possible. We didn't fit.
obstinate, I refused to accept and
proposed anyway
quilting our memories warm and fuzzy
role playing ninjitsu from Naruto, playing
Smash Bros for hours, I always losing, but you
teaching me never to give up. The
umbrage we experienced with
very tough career choices
we carried each other through -
ex I never imagined calling you.
youthful glow of camaraderie we shared, but the
zeal to remain afloat faded

## stray

falling in love with you
my best friend felt effortless
like melting unlimited
cotton candy on my tongue

you accepted my pop rocks personality
in return your dependable trustworthiness
was addicting as deep fried oreos

strolling hand in hand on the boardwalk
my comfortable confidant,
you were my safety vest
but you couldn't curb my carnival desire
chasing roller coasters

## yearn

routine drenched my skies
in dismal unyielding fog
when his vivacious spirit
streaked across like a shooting star
I didn't know I was wishing for

swiftly he became
the sun illuminating my days
glowing warmth I enjoy basking in
his presence in my life -
regaling radiant adventures
with flaring seal bark gusto -
I utmostly covet

## gravitate

in the haze of flickering laser lights
and reverberating techno thumps
your hands encircled my waist
to be one, but over your shoulder
I saw him alone, truly one
headbanging in fiery passion
I bid adieu to my type A
to surf the cloud of ecstasy
his wordless philosophy
altered my DNA

when he and I
bump and collide
I am jolted alive
living in a kaleidoscope
my rapid heartbeats
a rhythm I cavort to

## falsify hope

your niggling intuition was right
when I stepped closer to the throng
on the dancefloor than you

inspired by his independence
liberation I sought from you
I didn't want to admit

still you offered me a life raft
to let me explore uncharted waters
destination less
I chose to remain anchored
neither of us wanted
to be friends with loneliness

## succumb

I adamantly dug my heels into the sand
alone I faced the wrath of Father Time
your pull flowed and ebbed
my tides of courage

I waited for your nightly visits
I withstood your lunar phases
I wondered if we could journey in unison
I wrote infinity symbols in your shadows

we endured
but in our triumph I was fatigued

his constellation of hope
became my north star
against your waning moonlight

# repeat history

you shopped at Tiffany & Co
while I cheered on Roman gladiators
by coincidence we met in a co-ed bathroom
washing hands, small talk
I was taken by your politeness
learning we belonged to the same writing club
a shining comparison to brash, drunk brutes
I'd try to see the best in
I wanted to know you more

he shopped at Cheers Wine & Spirits
while I cheered on my cat children
by coincidence we sat side by side
playing Catan on game night
I was smitten by his gentleman approach
learning we shared desire to feed curiosity
the stellar comparison to your silver tongue
I'd try to see past
I wanted to know him more

## muse

step one: overanalyze
in my deep REM state
he stumbled in
door left ajar
he frequented, captured
the spotlight of my heart
my mind left asunder
his starring role
outweighed our reality together
it wasn't fair to you
he was a bandaid
I couldn't shake off

step two: fantasize
he searched for an apartment
his guide, I tugged him along
we paused at the library, perusing
my choice Greek mythology
*I like this too*, he said
when family dysfunction interrupted
he consoled my outburst of disappointment
we watched the New York skyline
to celebrate his new bachelor pad
*I enjoy being around you.*
swinging me around, he kissed me
I was overtaken by a sense of belonging

it was a fictional lifetime, lifeline, timeline
in person, it wasn't guaranteed
just an acquaintance, just a crush
I'd still choose the chance, the risk-
him

## crave chaos

numerous obstacles we weathered
forbidden by family
long distance
commitment

disasters exerting pressure
under my umbrella I tugged you in
fighting our future forecast
I believed we could outlast

but then the howling hurricane blew in
you rushed to shutter the windows
while I stood doused in torrential rain
exhilarated

an inkling grew, storm chaser
I cried a monsoon missing him
over you, much to my vexation
I was the eye in our desolation

## conclude

part one: upend us
at the pinnacle of our five
Christmases spent together
you moved in with me
and took up a new hobby
of painting our ever after
sailing on calm waters
to the music of dolphin laughter
but a tempest brewed in my heart
I wanted to swim rather than be onboard
to an expected culmination

part two: betray
he was your friend
invited to our housewarming
you stepped onto the balcony
to smoke with other guests,while
he and I gotta know each other over shots
Cupid's antics instigated
our instant burgeoning connection
blame me for my fickle feelings
but I only tumbled from grace in your eyes
because I wasn't honest months prior
I didn't want to be on the pedestal you adored

## hurt you

*how could I have been*
*so wrong about you?*

*wish I knew*
*when your smile*
*became fake*

*were we ever*
*in love?*

*I trusted you*

## withhold

sixty hour work weeks
plus household chores
coming home to see you
in pjs in bed working on a laptop
struck me as ambitionless

constant chatter during the day
fractured my mental peace
coming home to see you
waiting, needing my attention
struck me as overwhelming

carving out a date night
meant planning ahead of time
coming home to see you
with a list of kinks than solutions
struck me as inhibiting fun ventures

talk about anything, share interests
but I preferred hugs over kisses
I didn't want to come home to you
sedulously avoiding your craving touch
struck me as the end of us

## lie

I confessed he plagued me
like a looping record with
a haunting melody

I named him the iceberg
that sunk our relationship
but I was honeying the truth

the way you explode
is the way I detonate
the way you panic
is the way I freak
the way you love - unabashedly
is the way I love - passionately

you are my mirror
how could I not accept you
instead I have to let you go
so we can both grow

## revolve

as you piece the shards of
your splintered soul
I do the same

*my dream girl*, you declared
the way you want me
is the way I want him

the way I step away from you
is the way he walks away from me
we're a cyclone of despair

## devastate all

before you,
I didn’t have a
constant reliability

I tell you my care
has changed form
and you still remain
trying to adapt
to my needs -

I don't deserve you
like I don't deserve him.

the one who has the
power to shatter
fragile and delicate endearment
doesn't deserve love at all

## rewind and reminisce

thirty four days after our breakup
twenty two days since I last saw you
seven days with no contact at all

we decided to check in
a video call to watch
our favorite shows at the same time

seeing you again
talking to you, hearing you
was like getting slammed in the face
with a freshly baked,warm apple pie
shocking and ooey-gooey

I didn't want to take my eyes off you
wondering-
my heart bleeding indigo
from love, shame, and nostalgia -
*did I make a mistake?*

I'd glad I got to see you carry yourself
like a professional actor
it reminded me of our good times
hikes and philosophical discussions
eating ramen to anime debuts
the teddy bear I wanted to sidle up to

after a laborious day

I still haven’t thrown out your toothbrush
I have your old flannel in my closet
the picture of us on my bedside
momentarily, the buzz of regret
swarmed my heart

we were a soft pillow our heads
ached to sink into at night
a luxury I didn't think I'd have
before you
my much needed support

a tear slipped
I lamented what we had
what I may never have again
but the second I doubted us
I wasn't true to us anymore

the right decision
bites like bitter Bacardi

## dupe

so mesmerized by his illusory
tricks to stay upbeat
I was convinced our magic
required too much strenuous effort

he always had a bouquet of
jovial words to pull from his hat
while you stumbled through
novelty practices

mentally I pitted the two of you
juxtaposed, while I disappeared
into a box, circumnavigating the truth
I don't recognize myself anymore

## lose balance

*a lot of little things,* I said
as the cause to us flatlining
but he tipped the scale
with the promise of getaways
I tried to clasp you consolingly
but my wandering mind
focused on forthcoming possibilities
my heart faltering
detracted my value
in your judgement

he was no better
*when will I see you again,* I asked
*literally whenever*, he responded
in the February chill, I turned to wave
he reciprocated in endearment
but when he shut the garage door
behind me, he locked it tight
my heart pining
detracted my value
in his judgement

## transform

I was never a belle
with seasonally manicured nails
sashaying in hot pink heels
I prefer combat boots to stomp in
dresses under piles of cardigans
always tied together with a men's coat
my rufescent frizzy mane
cascading down my shoulders

before him, I know you chose me
appreciative of my authentic style
to match my attitude

yet when he said, *you are beautiful*
I staggered
like a fool who downed too many
whiskey glasses, overconfidently
trusting in my new dalliance

but our embrace was fleeting
when he saw the scars under my layers
the ones that bolstered my
cavalier quips and brash risks
and upheld my ferocious inner Leo.

how is it the beast he saw
and ran from
is the one you can still pet and withstand
despite the verbal claw marks left behind?

## don a façade

staring at my apartment walls
pleasantly adorned with emblems of love
to inspire a new fairytale
I am overwhelmed with claustrophobia

all too soon you come for a visit
all too soon you impersonate him
all too soon you try to rekindle what was
all too soon I am imprisoned by your proximity

you are everything I know
a deep baritone lullaby
serenading, dissolving, my hesitance
hypnotized I oblige to concurring
we could be a family again

but your graze turns insistent
jarring me out of my lulled reverie
of the future I stole from us
remembering my happiness
is not contingent to pleasing you

you pull me in
*I miss him*, I think
I pull back
*I still miss him*

you register my glumness
you interrogate me even
but I do not need the wrath
of your disapproval
when I am heart sore
mourning the ghost of him

mum and tight lipped
because you have no right
to explain or downplay
how I feel -why I let embers
of his memories warm me

you're just
not
the one

neither is he

I am overwhelmed by comprehension
I will not have an epic ballad
about my quintessential relationship
my walls now are much too high to overcome

## believe me

I didn't mean to.
like a kite caught in a gust of wind
my heart blew away
if I'd held tighter, would we still be together?

*you only have one choice,* you said
*choose me.*

like indulging in comfort food
your existence was reassuring
soothing teas, soft blankets, a security in life

meanwhile he made me burst
like a volatile firecracker
long drives, loud music, a lust for life

he doesn't want to be my choice
he shouldn't be

right now, I need to create a
reflection I like seeing

sometimes it feels like falling into oblivion
I cannot envision not knowing you
I cannot fathom not meeting him
impacted I am by flashing burgundy qualms

who am I without either of you?
I have to choose me.

www.ingramcontent.com/pod-product-compliance
Lightning Source LLC
La Vergne TN
LVHW020535160826
845677LV00015B/4067

* 9 7 8 9 3 5 7 2 1 0 0 9 6 *